# PERSONAL DEVELOPMENT

## Coloring Book
## with life lessons

*(But not all, like, preachy...)*

# for kids!!

*(And adults too I guess....*
*...cause, they can help with the coloring.)*

"Why am I Mr. Pink?

Why can't we pick our own colors?"

- Mr. Pink

# Life is a journey...

## ...enjoy the moments along the way!

Sometimes when we're going somewhere,
we only think about *where* we are going.

Don't forget to see and enjoy what is on the way.

# Accept yourself,

# love yourself,

# know that you are great!

You are special, unique and beautiful.

There is only one of you...
            ...and you are perfect just the way you are.

# Write down your goals and dreams.

Write down the things you want to do and have.

Writing down your goals helps them come alive!

# Do what you like to do!

Follow your passions.

You will enjoy doing things that are your passion.

# Make mistakes.

Mistakes help you learn.

You are not a failure if you make a mistake.

You are learning how to be sucessful!

# Learn from other people.

If you want to know how to do something ask, or watch, someone who knows how to do it.

You will learn and they will be happy to teach!

# Read.

## Read.

### Read.

Books can change your life!

# Give thanks.

Be thankful for everything good you have, and everything you like.

Thank people who have done things for you - your parents, your granny, a teacher.

# Keep a journal.

Write down what's going on in your head and your heart.

It helps you stay in touch with yourself,
and can keep your thoughts and feelings clear.

# Confess, and don't make excuses.

If you do something wrong, or make a mistake, be honest.

Everything will be okay.

# Take risks!

Take the risk to try something new...

...or to talk to someone you like...

...or to get something you want.

# Things don't make you happy.

Happiness is on the inside, not the outside.

But it's okay to want stuff.

# Learn to be patient.

Sometimes we don't get what we want right away.
Sometimes we have to wait.


Patience makes waiting easier,
and it is something you can practise.

# Write a list of all the things you want to do in life.

It's fun!!

# Challenge yourself.

Don't be afraid to try something difficult.

Give it a shot!

# Speak the truth.

Always try to tell the truth.

Say what you really mean.

# Communicate.

Say what you really want as clearly as possible.

That way you can avoid misunderstandings.

# Ask questions!

Ask more questions!

# Try not to gossip.

Try not to talk bad about other people or tell tales.

# Ask for help.

Don't be afraid to ask for help if you can't do something, or can't understand something.

It's not being weak...it's being strong.
It's not being dumb...it's being smart.

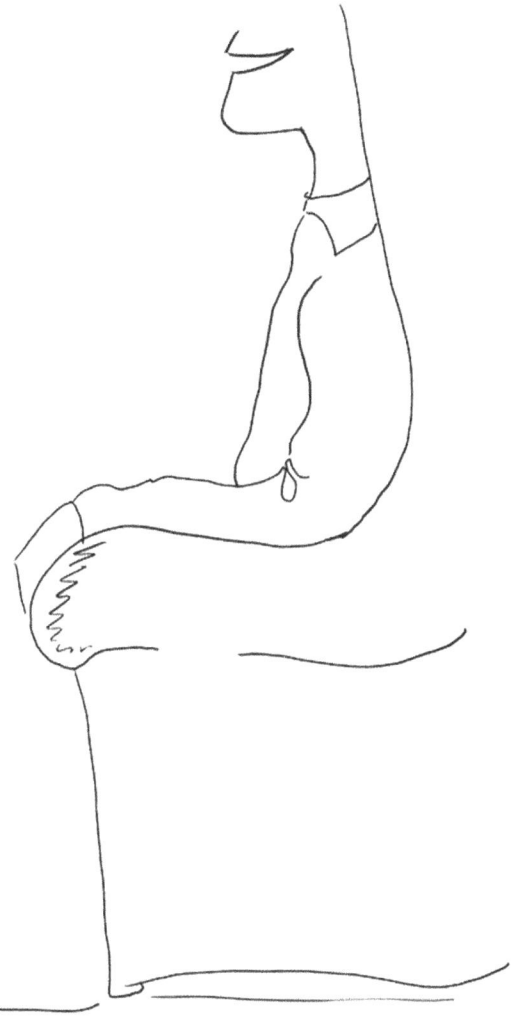

# Positive thoughts become positive things!

Negative thoughts become negative things.
Try to look for the best in any situation.


Try to be optimistic!

# Try not to complain.

The more you complain, the worse things become!

# Don't take anything personally.

The stuff people do or say isn't your fault.

If you can ignore bad things people say to you then they can't hurt you.

# Don't stop...never give up!

If you want to do something, or achieve something, never give up!

Some things are easy - some things take time and hard work.

Often it's just when we want to stop that we should keep going.

# Keep your promises!

(Especially promises you make to yourself.)

People will respect you and trust you.

# Accept that some things change.

Everything in the world is always changing…
…this is something we just can't stop.

Sometimes if you don't want something to happen, it makes it even harder to get through what is happening.

Learn to accept things that are not in your control.

# Ask for forgiveness.

Say sorry to someone if you think that you did something wrong.


It's okay...say that you're sorry.

# Be forgiving.

Forgive anyone who hurts you.

They don't mean it, they are just trying not to hurt themselves.

If you forgive them...
          ...it means that they cannot hurt you.

# Draw a monkey here!